Pearls

Protect Your Most Valuable Thing

by
Lakeisha K. Carey

Cover designed by Self-Publishing Services
Editing and Layout by Self-Publishing Services

Printed in the United States of America

Library of Congress Control Number: 2022911196
Published in Chesapeake, Virginia

Print ISBN - 979-8-9864443-0-7
Ebook ISBN - 979-8-9864443-1-4

CONTENTS

PEARLS

Protect Your Most Valuable Thing

LaKeisha K. Carey

ACKNOWLEDGMENTS

This book has truly been a journey. I want to start this acknowledgment off by thanking My Lord, Father God, His son Jesus Christ for dying for me so that I can be healed and walk in my healing and wholeness and the Holy Spirit who is with me daily!

I'm grateful for my Husband who has pushed me to write this book and supported me throughout my journey. Thanks to my three little arrows, I pray they don't have to go through any of the things I went through.

Special thanks to my sweet, sweet daddy, God bless his soul as He Rest In Peace. Thanks for always being their daddy! Special thanks to my mommy who is a testament of God's healing and redemption. I'm forever grateful for our relationship, how we have healed from the past, made a true effort to be intentional with our love and support for one another! I love you lady forever!

Thank you to my Spiritual Fathers, mothers, and mentors. Robbie Cade Furdge and Latoya JT Jackson, the way y'all have loved me, prayed for me, supported and pushed me has been beyond words. Y'all are truly God-sent. Also, the hand y'all had in this book has been everything. Thank you, I appreciate you!

Special thanks to two of my close friends Jessica Harris and Quemeka Riviera who read this book and provided me their unbiased feedback. God showed one of them the vision for the cover and the name of this book! They are truly connected to me! I love y'all!

Lastly, thank you to all my family, friends, and supporters! I don't take for granted of anyone who purchase this book, I'm truly grateful and appreciate you! This book was created and written for a certain audience and my only hope that it get into the hands of that audience FOR GOD's Glory! So thank you and enjoy!

Introduction

Thank you! Thank you! Thank you for buying and picking up my book to read it. In this book, you will find my journey, my testimony, and my road to healing. I have to be honest with you. I started writing this book in March 2021 and wanted to have it published and in your hands in August for my 35th birthday. But around June/July as I was hashing out some things in this book, I put it down and took a sabbatical. It got really heavy! I felt the need to finish, but I also felt the pressure of, Am I sharing too much? What are people going to think? Will this really help someone? All of the negative self-talk.

But can I say, God will put a pushing on you and send some people to speak over your life and get you back on track. So I picked this back up in September and sent what I had to the publishing company. The feedback the publisher gave me pushed me to complete this because I could see how much this book was needed. Not only that when I would scroll on social media or speak to some young ladies, I realized I was not just writing this book for nothing. There was a specific audience that needed every word on each page.

I mention all of that to say, you are about to enter into a real, raw, uncut version of my life. This is my testimony, this was my journey, and I AM a SURVIVOR of many battles. BUT I only survived because of my Heavenly Father and my Savior. I lived to tell the story. And GOD gave me the title to this book, *Pearls: Protect Your Most Valuable Thing*, when I was in the midst of casting. This title came from a scripture reference in Matthew, and it was moment when Jesus was speaking on the Mount.

In Matthew 7:6, KJV: "Give not that which is holy unto the dogs, neither cast ye your pearls before swine, lest they trample them under their feet, and turn again and rend you."

This scripture and the message behind it to me meant "do not waste valuable time giving valuable things to those who will not appreciate it." When we look at the wild animals in the text, it's not talking about your normal pets but dangerous, filthy, unclean, immoral creatures. This scripture was a warning. Jesus did not want his people to give their pearls to swine or pigs because pigs were too dumb to understand what a pearl is WORTH!!!! I could drop the mic right there and stop writing because this book is all about not giving up the valuable, worthy things in our lives, whether that is our knowledge or information, our time, our relationships, our energy, or ourselves.

Let me say this: I am not calling anyone a swine or a pig, LOL. I am using this metaphor for the swine- and pig-like experiences, circumstances, and traumas I endured and how I cast my pearls not realizing their worth or my worth. Also, I want to stress how the enemy is tricky yet subtle, and his devices are used to kill, steal, and destroy us BUT GOD!!!!.

I do want to put a disclaimer here. In this book, some heavy issues will be discussed, such as different type of abuse (sexual and domestic), toxic relationships, and a lot of brokenness and pain, so if reading this book triggers some things for you, I apologize in advance. My hope that this book will not trigger but help you deal with past, present, and even future concerns so you can walk in wholeness and healing.

Before we get started, I do want to take some time to discuss how pearls are prepared and why they are so valuable. Pearls are one of the most valuable, one-of-a-kind, earth's prized possession. Pearls are created as a defense mechanism. When an oyster encounters an irritant, it responds by surrounding the invader with layers of translucent but solid material called nacre. The irritant, whether it's an innocuous grain of sand or a more deadly parasite, is isolated and made harmless.

In the ancient world, pearl diving was a hard and dangerous occupation. The most prized pearls were the perfectly spherical ones. A diver had to collect as much as three tons of oysters to find just three or four spherical pearls worthy of the royals who sought them.

At one point, pearls were among the most expensive possessions in the world.

Even though we've discovered ways to cultivate pearls, their existence is still a bit of a miracle. Production of quality pearls is a delicate process with no guarantee of success.

Then, once they are harvested, there's still quite a bit of work involved in making sure their natural beauty is on full display. Before pearls are sold, they are prepared. The preparation process is divided into five steps. Those steps include finishing, which is when the pearl is soaked to rid it of unwanted residue. In the second step, the pearls are sorted by shape, size, and grade to determine their value. Then, craftsmen carefully drill through to make sure the pearl has the perfectly aligned holes. Finally, because each pearl is unique and no two pearls are exactly the same, they must be matched. This process is time consuming because the matcher sorts through thousands of pearls to find another of the same size, shape, and luster. The last step in preparing the pearls is threading the gemstone on the strands. A fully matched string of pearls (at least in Jesus' time) represented literally several years worth of wages and work.

It amazes me how you will see a little of this process in each chapter.

Let's not waste any time, let's dive in!

1. In the Midst

Have you ever prayed for something you knew was not conducive for you? I knew the relationship I was in was toxic, not good for me, not producing good fruits, stagnated, and I was losing me! But I still wanted it and prayed for it.

Before I go further, let me take it back to the beginning.

When I first met him—let's call him John Doe—I was flattered by his swag, and he was smooth with his words. It started off by flirting with each other, and then we exchanged numbers. He was so sweet and funny. We started spending serious time with each other, like every day, and finally put a title of boyfriend and girlfriend on our relationship. I fell in love with his sense of humor, his dreams, and his potential.

While we were in a relationship, I noticed he was always with one of his boys, and there were always different females around. When we had conversations about his past relationships, he would talk about his crazy ex-girlfriend. But this crazy ex-girlfriend would still pop up from time to time. (Red flag, maybe she wasn't crazy and he was still entertaining her). I trusted his word that she was his ex.

After being in a relationship for a year or so, I noticed he started lying about his whereabouts, lying about the people, especially girls, who were hanging around, and lying about small things. Also, when we would have disagreements, it would always escalate to name-calling and us calling it quits.

Now if I'm honest, I would get so mad that I would always threaten to break up first. We really did not know how to handle conflict. (Another red flag).

After about three or four years, the cycle never changed. There was always a new rumor of him messing with a new girl, and our relationship was stagnated. We tried to do long distance, but there was no trust. It felt like we were just going through the motions. I was giving so much but losing myself in the midst. We would break up, get back together, and break up again.

One particular night, I visited my daddy's house in my hometown. I tried reaching out to John Doe about my safe arrival. He did not answer my calls or text. He was not working, and this was not the first time he had ignored my calls. I had a gut feeling something was not right. I called his mother's house; she hadn't seen him either. The next day, when he did call back, he lied about falling asleep at his mom's. Clearly, he did not know I had already spoken to his mother. I hung up the phone pissed.

In the midst, I was sitting on the floor, crying begging, pleading, and wrestling with my desire to stay in this toxic relationship with this man, and that is when God birthed the title of this book in me. **Don't cast your pearls amongst swine**.

According to Merriam-Webster dictionary, in the midst means "during or in the middle of something." That can include a toxic relationship, a spiritual battle, or war, just anything where you are not at the start or the end of it. I titled this chapter "In the Midst" because I was in the middle of a relationship when I received this title. I knew I was in the middle because I was far from the beginning and not quite at the end...in the midst.

Listen, God will speak while we are in the midst of bad situations, but we have to discipline ourselves to hear and obey.

I wondered, when God gave me this title, was He trying to give me a glimpse of His purpose so I would chose to leave, or was He actually showing me what my actions were doing to me? I did not listen and willfully disobeyed. As a consequence, I spent years stuck in a bad situation and suffered hurt after hurt.

Things did not seem that bad during the relationship. I saw that this relationship had the potential to be a great thing. I saw the good traits, and those traits blinded me from seeing the red flags. When I saw the flags, or someone else tried to tell me about them, I did not take heed but shunned the actual people who saw the blind spots and tried to warn me.

In all honesty and in essence, I became toxic too! It wasn't good for either one of us to be with one another. I still remember when my Pastor at the time called me out on my toxic behavior. We were all out eating, and in conversation I was talking recklessly toward John Doe and belittling him. At this time, I was with him but I reminded him daily that I did not need him and could be with anybody else. He got up and went to the bathroom, and Pastor Demars asked me why I spoke to him the way I did. I really didn't know what he meant. That was just the way I communicated.

He said, "You are addressing him from a hurt, bitter, resentful, angry place, and you need to change that." He went on to say, "If you have to speak to him in that manner, you do not need to be with him." He also said that regardless of my hurt and feelings, John Doe was still a king and child of Christ, and I should address him as such!

I did not realize I was doing this until he called me out on it. But this moment changed the trajectory of my communication with men. I vowed to never speak, belittle, or downgrade another man, I would speak and address the king in him because regardless of how I felt, I needed to see him as a king and a child of God!

Now lets me be real—this is hard because when a man has

hurt you, you are not thinking about these principles and definitely not trying to put them in play But GOD will challenge you to know and do better. I wanted to start putting this advice in action.

I wanted this relationship to work so badly. However, I allowed a lot of things to happen, and I grew numb to the lies, the hurt, and the unchanged behavior. I failed to set a standard or boundaries in the beginning, so he knew what he could get away with. He knew the right words to say so I would continue to stay with him and not require any significant changes from him.

The last straw for me was when my girlfriend called and told me that he was on a date with another girl, and she had evidence to prove it. I finally decided I needed to be done even though I loved him. At this moment, I needed my mind and heart to line up and my feet to match the actions.

While in the midst, I learned two important things: God wanted better for me; and I could not afford to give up In the Midst. I also learned that I got in the midst by ignoring red flags, not setting healthy boundaries, not hearing wise counsel, staying longer than I should, and believing in the potential.

Once I made the decision to end the relationship, I felt like I would never go back, and I was strong enough to still entertain him, talk to him, and even stay in contact. That was an epic failure because I was back in it before I knew it. "My feelings battled God's will." I was leaning more towards, "I love him!" And I was turning away from the sound counsel of God. This man was symbolically my right arm. He was so much a part of my life, he seemed essential, and dare I say irreplaceable. But as the Lord said in the book of Matthew, "if your right arm offends you, cut it off."

In order for me to truly heal, I knew I had to cut the ties, block the number, block social media, burn pictures and gifts. I took a spiritual sabbatical for months where God and I took a journey. He started revealing my brokenness, and He started stripping things away. The healing truly started.....

I cannot end this chapter without discussing signs of toxic relationships and some practical steps to get out. Looking back, some of the toxic signs were toxic communication—the inability to talk to one another without name-calling, belittling, and cussing each other out. Another sign was dishonesty and a pattern of disrespect. It was the disappearing acts and the habitual lying even about small things. The last sign was the lack of trust and lack of changed behavior. I gave years of my life in this relationship, and there were no significant changes in his behavior, in our relationship, in my actions, and no trust.

I want to encourage those who may be in the midst of a bad situation, DO NOT SETTLE in it. Sometimes you have to take drastic measures to get drastic results. You may need to block the access to yourself, burn up things that will remind you, and replace your time with something productive.

The reality is that it is going to hurt when you leave and you may feel like the hurt is overbearing, but God can heal you and the hurt. Search scriptures about healing and what God thinks of you! Remind yourself of those words and your value and worth, and take the time out to truly heal before getting into another relationship.

Lastly, you need some accountability partners who can tell you truth, pray with you, and walk with you. These people cannot be afraid to tell you what's real, and when they do, you should not shun them. These people need to be healed and whole and have a personal relationship with Christ. They need to be able to reach heaven with their prayers and release faith that the chains can be broken off your life!

Know that the chains can be broken! We serve a God who has conquered death, He can conquer anything you are facing, and He can help you be set free and free indeed!

- Do not settle or give up in the midst. It is easy to get comfortable and settle, especially when you have given yourself and your time and lost yourself. BUT it is okay to start over. It may be hard but you got this.
- Recognize the Red Flags. So many times, we can be blinded by love, like, or even lust that we ignore toxic or unhealthy behavior and find ourselves stuck for years.
- Set healthy boundaries. In all of your relationships especially romantic, set boundaries, and healthy ones. If there are no boundaries, so many lines will be crossed with no consequences to follow. Set those boundaries in the beginning. Connect with your support systems to develop your boundaries.

Notes

_____

_____

_____

_____

_____

_____

_____

_____

_____

_____

_____

_____

Prayer

Dear Heavenly Father,

We come to you humbly yet boldly. Thank you for not allowing me to die in the midst. Forgive me for every moment that I did not take heed to your voice or your commandments. God, please help me not to settle or give up while in an unhealthy situation. God, please help me to set healthy boundaries in all of my relationships and not ignore any red flags.

God, I am really standing in the gap for those who have settled because they have grown weary. God, I pray for their strength. You said in your word that your power is perfected in our weakness (2 Corinthians 12:9). God, I cover the one who is reading this and feeling broken, tired, hurt, lost trust, and hope. My prayer is that You stand in the gap, comfort them, and help them to totally put their trust in You, for You will never fail them nor leave or forsake them. Holy Spirit minister to every broken and hurt place and restore their joy, their love, their trust, their faith. God, open their eyes to see their relationships for what they are and not what they desire them to be. Give them the ability to seek you in their healing and identify the toxic patterns in their own thought processes, minds, bodies, and souls. Help them to lay it all at your feet. Change them like only you can, God!

In your matchless name, Jesus, I pray.

Amen

2. WOUNDED

What does it mean to be wounded? Wounded is defined as inflicted with a wound; injured. I've rewritten this chapter more than once because I wanted to go deeper in how I was wounded. Several things in my childhood wounded me, and those wounds caused me to grow up with insecurities, abandonment, rejections, and even problems with the way I viewed love and men. The wounds started with being raised by my dad.

Single fathers are far less common than **single mothers**, constituting 16% of **single-parent families**. According to Single Parent Magazine, the number of **single fathers** has increased by 60% in the last ten years, and is one of the fastest growing family situations in the United States.

I want to start off by saying my mom and I are in a much better place. We have an amazing relationship, but in order for me to walk in my healing, I have to tell where my initial hurt stemmed from.

When I was about six or seven and my sister was four or five, my mom and dad got into a huge argument, and my mom was trying to leave. I do not know the details of what happened to get to this point. My dad was begging my mom to stay, but my mom did not want to. My mom got into the car to leave; she didn't pack us up to take us with her though. My dad told me and my sister to jump on the car so she would not leave. We jumped on the car to stop her from leaving. But that did not stop her, She left anyway. Soon thereafter, my dad filed for divorce because they couldn't work it out. When it came to the custody arrangement, we remained with our dad.

I'm not saying things were perfect between my parents and they did not have their irreconcilable differences. I am saying my sister and I would have loved to be able to have a full relationship with both parents. Divorce is hard. It's an attack from the enemy to divide families, and it takes a different toll on the children who are in the families. The divorce ripped away a part of what we knew to be normal. During this time of separation, we were disappointed a lot because we would get excited about going to stay with our mom and then some things would come up where she couldn't make it. We experienced a lot of broken promises. And then we had to go through spending time in different places, we had to adjust to the stepparent life, and transition with the changes.

When I was around the age of seven or eight, my mom started a new relationship with a new man. This was her new home, now this man became her abuser. When we would visit, we would see him hurt her. She could not protect us from being hurt by him. He would curse at her, call her names, push her, and beat her. It started to feel like it would happen every time we would come to visit. Like they were fighting because of us. It got to a point where he beat her so bad, my sister and I ran to the neighbor's house and called the police. When they came, my mom and stepdad both denied what had happened and made up a different story. He told my mom we could not visit anymore. And we didn't come for a while to let everything "calm down." This man had broken my mom's bones, busted her eye vessels, and really abused her bad.

You would think abusing my mom was enough. Nope! He started being verbally abusive to us. And then he started to make me do inappropriate things, too. From sitting on his lap to play driving while he enjoyed it to other sexual things. He would wait until my mom would leave to work the night shift to make his move. I was so young, only nine or ten, and did not have any idea of what I was being asked to do. But he took advantage of my innocence and exploited it for his personal gains. He became my abuser, too. We (my mom or me) were not safe in his presence. He threatened me to never speak of the abuse that occurred, his inappropriateness, and I did not because I was afraid.

I was so hurt because I felt my mom could not protect me. I was broken, but in reality, my mom was broken, too. He manipulated her, he controlled her, and he broke her. She endured domestic abuse and other abuse for 13-plus years.

This hurt made me have a strong disgust for my mom. I resented her. I became disrespectful. My little mind just couldn't understand why she left our home in the first place, and why my parents had to get divorced. Not only that, but why would she leave to be with a man who abused her. Why would she leave to be with a man who abused me, too!

Finally, I mustered the guts to tell my mom. I remember like it was yesterday. We were at one of their friend's houses at a party. I told her what he did to me; she was hurt and believed me, but she did not know how she could get out of this abusive relationship. She stayed. He continued to manipulate and control her. This hurt me again.

All of this hurt made me feel rejected and abandoned because I felt like I was unworthy and could not be loved. I felt insecure because I struggled with thoughts like, *Am I enough?* and *Why am I not enough?* I battled with my self-esteem because I felt like a huge part of my life was missing. I did not know myself and my value. I felt the very thing God had given me was not protected. I felt like my mom was not protected either.

Most people would have stayed here and took on the victim mentality, and if it was not for the grace of God on my life, I would have also. But what I'm about to say next is a testimony on how God healed me. If you are someone who is still dealing with wounds, whether from divorce, a single-parent home, sexual abuse, church hurt, or etc, my prayer is that you would ask God to heal you as he did me and countless others who sought His love.

After carrying this hurt for a while, I had a supernatural experience. I was about 12 years old, and I was in the backseat of my mom's car. God told me I needed to forgive her. At 12, I really did not understand the ins and outs of forgiveness. But I did know when someone did something wrong to you, if they apologized, you would say, "I forgive you," and move on. This was a little different because no one apologized but God still wanted me to do it. I'll never forget—it felt like God touched my heart and allowed me to do it. In that moment, I forgave my mom, and I even forgave her significant other. This was the beginning of the healing journey. Forgiveness, true forgiveness, is the beginning stage of the healing process.

Even though I forgave, I still experienced a sense of rejection, abandonment, and insecurities. I found myself doing the bare minimum with my relationship with my mom. I was respectful, but I was not in a place of honoring her. I was not taking any initiative to show in my actions that I honored her and appreciated her. This took a much longer time. I still remember when God helped me to release my mom and the hurt in my adult life.

It was 2013, and my husband and I were doing marriage counseling with Bishop Robert and Pastor Betty Cade. In our session, we discussed childhood and honoring our parents. Pastor Betty said, "You cannot be a great mother or wife without first honoring your mother, plus your days on earth will be longer."

This resonated in me. I realized I was not making a real effort to honor my mom. Honor means to show positive regard for parents through words and behaviors. "While honor is an internal attitude of respect, courtesy, and reverence, it should be accompanied by appropriate attention or even obedience. Honor without such action is incomplete;

it is lip service." (Baker's Bible Dictionary) But from that day forward, I started being intentional with my interactions with my mom. I was intentional with checking in on her, respecting her, and showing her love. When we had our differences, I handled it not out of irritation but with a spirit of love! That's why I can now say our relationship has truly grown and matured. My mom is truly active in my life and my children's lives. I can see the growth and healing in her, and we can have deeper conversations. I'm forever grateful for our process and our growth.

The true testimony of all of this is my mommy found her voice and courage to leave an abusive situation and she is a survivor. I'm grateful to God that He kept her and allow her to get out. She is truly my hero for not allowing an abusive relationship to stop her! I'm glad she is still here to share her story! I'm forever grateful that she is an amazing mother and grandmother. My life wouldn't be the same without her. Thanks mom!

I've learned even in estranged relationships there are ways you can still be honorable to your parents. If you have experienced a difficult situation with your parents, my advice would be to forgive. Though forgiveness can be hard, it's worth it. I would also pray about ways you can honor your parents. I understand everyone's situation is different, and I'm not telling you to push yourself in a situation or a pattern where you are abused or hurt. I just do not want you to be walking in an unforgiveness state.

Also, if you are a parent, please protect your children. Discern the company you keep and the company your kids are around. When your kids encounter tough situations and confide in you about it, believe them. Not only believe them, let your actions show that you believe them. I remember being so afraid to tell my daddy about what happened. Not that I could not share with him anything, but I was afraid of what he would do to the abuser.

If your children have encountered some type of abuse or trauma, please get them some counseling. It's never too early to start counseling, and it's imperative so they can deal with what they have experienced now rather than suppress it and have to deal with it plus more as an adult.

- Divorce does not only impact the two people who are getting it but it impacts the children and others. Be godly sure before saying, I do!
- Know the company that is around your children, protect them, cover them in prayer, and teach them about the appropriate and inappropriate touches.
- Honor your parents. The command does not give excuses or reason when this is not to be done which in essence mean Honor is beyond your feelings and thoughts, it is a must!

Notes

_____

_____

_____

_____

_____

_____

_____

_____

_____

_____

_____

_____

_____

_____

Prayer

Dear Abba Father,

Thank you so much for being such an example of how our earthly relationship should look with our parents. Help us to Honor you and Honor our earthy parents. Help us to forgive them for anything that they have done, and help us to love them.

God, this was a heavy chapter, and there are so many people who have endured divorce, abuse, whether physical, emotional, or sexual, and the feelings of abandonment, rejection, and personal insecurities. God, I pray that no one is taking the blame or feels like the abuse that happened to them is their fault. Help them to release the guilt and shame. Help those who are crying out to you because the weight of life is feeling too heavy. Help them not throw in the towel but know that you have a plan for their lives and even their story. Lord, we know the thoughts have you towards them, thoughts of peace, not of evil, and to give them an expected end (Jeremiah 29:11).

God, we lay all of these things at your feet and pray that you send your healing power. God, whatever we may have experienced in our lives, remind us that you care about us, and your word tells us to cast all of our cares on you, for you care (1 Peter 5:7). Thank you for caring.

God, I pray that you restore families. Restore Fathers in the home and Restore Mothers in the home. Our homes need You. Our children need You. We thank you for bringing Your Order back to the Homes.

In Jesus Name,

Amen

3. A Similar Situation

Being young and broken can cause you to forget about your value and succumb to another's perceived value of you. After the experiences in my childhood, it took years to deal with the layers of hurt. I carried this burden for a long time. And even though I forgave my mom, my own pain was still heavy on my heart. Due to this hurt, I found myself in a similar situation as my mom. I was so young and hadn't really been in any serious relationships. Nor, had I seen a lot of healthy relationships either.

Before heading to college, I met this guy (let's call him Adam). Adam and I were pretty involved with school activities in high school and had hoped to do great as students working towards our goals in getting into college. We had some similar interests and both wanted to work hard to make our families proud. We eventually decided to take our friendship to the next level and started dating. Now Adam was a really cool guy in the beginning. I couldn't tell you if there were any red flags or any warning signs initially. But then the real him began to show up.

Adam began to take serious interest in my hobbies and daily routines. He began popping up at my job every day and multiple times during the day. He started being very manipulative. He wanted to control everything I did, from the places I could or could not go, to the activities I could or could not participate in. He wanted me to be around him all the time. This became a pattern! At first, I thought it was cute. I thought, *He is just really into me.* But then it started to feel overwhelming. During this time, I stopped hanging around my friends and doing things I enjoyed. I found myself just doing what he wanted to do. Adam had successfully isolated me in the same way my mom was isolated.

Any time I would object to his demands, Adam became physically and verbally abusive. He would make me feel bad for wanting to do anything different. He really would break me down with his words and actions, but he still said he loved me. The longer I stayed in this relationship, the longer I was losing myself. My family and friends wanted me out, but I did not know how to get out. I was stuck.

This man even wanted to marry me. He bought a ring. He planned out this whole proposal in front of people we loved. Many of them had no clue the things I was going through. Because I was so ashamed to tell. As he was doing his spill about marrying me, it was another tactic to get me to stay so he could control me. I knew I was not ready to be married. And I knew that I did not need to marry him. But I did not want to embarrass him by saying no in front of everyone. I said yes.

Can we just stop right here and thank God for keeping us even when we don't want to be kept? Lord, I thank you for always making an escape route according to your word in 1 Corinthians 10:13 that you will provide the way of escape!

After being in this relationship with Adam for over a year, his insecurities grew stronger. Especially since we were "engaged!" We left for college and were in a new area. We did not move in together. We had our own separate places. He really tried to limit my free time and my whereabouts. I remember being so miserable because I was a pretty sociable person, but I did not socialize at all. My roommate was worried about me. Because she knew the truth. She had caught me crying several time because of his abuse.

Adam tried to keep me from doing any extracurricular activities. He did not want to run the risk of me enjoying anything else other than himself. I would literally go to class and back to my room. And when I got to my room, Adam would be right there waiting for me to get out of class. I honestly don't think he went to class because he was so worried about my schedule. Or if he did, he made sure to set his schedule in a way that allowed him to monitor mine.

Somewhere along the way, Adam found himself a new victim. He started messing with this other girl while we were together. I caught wind of it, but it wasn't until after the girl sought me out that I found out the truth. This was my escape route. I made some dumb mistakes by staying when it was just me. But I couldn't fathom continuing to make the same mistakes with other people involved. The other woman thought she was coming to check me about her man, but she was getting me out of a bad situation. This was my escape route, and I took it. I got out and was not looking back. Yes, he tried to come back, but I was not having it. The moment I got out of the relationship and I got a glimpse of freedom, I was not looking back.

You would think after seeing my mom go through this, I would have seen the warning signs and ran. No, instead I found myself in a similar situation.

Before ending this chapter, I have to say domestic abuse is never okay, and staying in an abusive relationship to save face is not either. If you are reading this and find yourself in an abusive relationship, please get some help[1]. You may not be strong enough to do it on your own, but there are resources out there to help you get to a safe place.

Also, though you may feel stuck, do not miss the escape route or the opportunity God provides for you to get out. I'm

---

[1] National Domestic Violence Hotline 800-799-7233
https://www.thehotline.org/

forever grateful that when the opportunity presented itself, I took it.

I want to encourage you that you don't deserve the abuse. Please do not think you can change your abuser because the reality is, even if you could change him, you could never change him the way God can or as good as God can. Get out and allow God to heal you and heal and change the other person. God has the King's hearts in His hand and can turn it as He pleases. I pray that you turn that person over to God and allow Him to deal with them.

After being in an abusive relationship, it may be wise to seek counseling. You will need help to build you back up and get your voice back.

Be conscious of the people you entertain, don't allow anyone to misuse or abuse you! Please get help!

Pearls of wisdom

- Abuse is real! There are different versions of abuse whether emotional, verbal (belittling, degrading, reckless words), mental/psychological, sexual, and physical. When you are in an abusive relationship, you feel like you cannot get out of it alone. Please use resources listed and get help. It's okay to need and get help. It's not your fault and you DO NOT DESERVE IT! (Resources: National Domestic Violence Hotline https://www.thehotline.org/)
- I challenge you after experiencing such a traumatic situation, please seek counseling and find ways to build yourself up and strengthen your values, esteem, and voice.
- TRUST yourself and the signs of abuse. When a person shows you their abusive behavior, get help and get out quickly, please. Don't think you can change them.

Notes

_____

_____

_____

_____

_____

_____

_____

_____

_____

_____

_____

_____

_____

Prayer

Dear Daddy,

God, thank you for allowing me to get out and survive from an abusive relationship. I know what I felt when I was in it, so I want to cover every person who may find themselves in a similar situation or who got out of a similar situation. I pray for their heart, mind, and strength. After experiencing abuse for any amount of time, you feel low in esteem, in value, and strength. You feel like you lost your voice and you just want it back. I pray for your children, restore them the joy of their salvation (Psalm 51:12), strengthen their value and spirit. Remind them that they are MORE THAN Conquerors (Romans 8:37) and they are wonderfully and fearfully made (Psalm 139:14). Please take away the guilt and shame they feel for being in such a relationship. Remind them it's not their fault and they should forgive themselves. Give them the spirit of discernment to test the spirit by your spirit and if these behaviors show up in word, action, or deed, that they get out fast. Please put support systems around them to uplift, protect, and help them.

God, I pray that no more lives are taken away due to abuse. I pray that at the point of any relationship if a person feels like they have to belittle, hit, batter, or downgrade, help both parties to cut the ties, because it's not worth it. Thank you, God, for being close to the brokenhearted and giving your peace, strength, and love to them.

To the one who created and loves us, we bless you.

In Jesus name,

Amen!

4. Cycle of Bad Relationships

I wish I could say, "This was the end of me casting my pearls before swine," but this was only the beginning. Though I got out of that abusive relationship, I was still broken and had not healed. I was in and out of relationships, trying to find the validation and the self-worth that was missing. But it did not help. I was not protecting the valuable things God gave me.

Sometimes we can get so used to being in something that the fear of starting over or letting go will keep us in an unhealthy situation for years. My situation became a vicious cycle of being in and out of damaging relationships with the wrong men, breaking up and starting over with hopes that the next time would be different. Doing the same thing and expecting a different result...Insanity!! In order to get over a failed and bad relationship, I found myself spending time with and in relations with people who I knew were not the one for me or good for me, knew it would not be anything serious, and it wasn't going to amount anything. I was wasting time and energy and honestly just going through the motions.

But nothing changed because I never healed or required changed behavior. I never set up the boundaries.

After the abusive relationship with Adam and the cyclical relationship with John Doe in Chapter 1, I did not want to be in another long-term relationship, especially anything serious.

During this time, I also decided to rededicate my life to

Christ. I stopped going out and got plugged in to this local church. I started serving and was in a good place in my life. I even got connected to this amazing group of young adults who loved God and were living for Him.

One of the guys who was a part of the group was interested in me. We became good friends and later decided to give the relationship thing a try. It was a new and beautiful thing because we both were doing this relationship God's way. We wanted to please God with all of our hearts, even our relationship.

Now this relationship could have been the "one" because the guy was truly a breath of fresh air from God. But because I did not completely deal with all of me and allowed some toxic traits to remain, I messed that thang ALL UP. I ended up going back to Old. It's so funny when you know something isn't good for you but your flesh desires it, and if you haven't disciplined yourself or your flesh, or even made up in your mind that you choose you and God's will for you, YOU WILL FALL or go BACK!!

I'll never forget how it happened. I was genuinely happy because I felt like I was really done with John Doe. But we ended up in the same place at the same time after not seeing each other for years. He wanted to talk, and I felt like I could handle this conversation. So we met up and talked. He was expressing his feelings and how much he missed me. He tugged on all of my heart strings. Before I knew it, I fell and fell hard. I cheated!

I ended up being truthful to my then boyfriend about what happened; he was heartbroken. I hurt him. I was hurt because I hurt him. How did I allow myself to go back? How did I allow myself to be in this situation? After all, I'd experienced so much hurt from broken relationships where someone cheated on me. Now I'd done the same thing to someone I cared for. I knew how it felt to be hurt, and now I had to deal with the fact I'd hurt someone else.

I have to say this, I thought I was above falling! I thought I was over it, but I wasn't. It's imperative for you to not put yourself in a position to fall! Don't think you're above it or strong enough in your own strength. The Bible says in 1 Corinthians 10:12, "Wherefore let him that thinketh he standeth take heed lest he fall!" (KJV)

I should not have set myself up in that position or predicament. It so important to not rely on your strength but God's, and to not put yourself in a position where you are going to be tempted! DO NOT allow yourself to fall for the "Baby, sorry, it will not happen again," and the sweet words. But instead look for the changed behavior and the changed heart.

Now it's been three failed relationships in the span of 10 years! How did I get here?

When you find yourself in and out of bad relationships, there comes a time when you have to do some evaluation and self-reflection. There is something in you that you need to heal from and be delivered from. You need to spend time with the Father asking the hard questions—why do I keep choosing this type of person, what is broken in me, how can I heal and learn my value, help me to see myself the way You do, and help me to never hurt another person.

Not only seek the Father, but wait until He answers. God is always speaking in different ways whether through His word or through people. We just have to be still long enough to allow Him to complete the work within us.

Also, there comes a time when we have to recognize and deal with the patterns. Those patterns can show up as changed behavior for a short period of time, then the same behavior returns. After you have been with someone who shows you the same patterns, you know it's time to seriously respond differently.

For me, I realized that there were still things I hadn't dealt with in me. I took on myself all the failed relationships and thought I was a failure. I also thought I deserved these things. My perspective had to change. I had to transform my mind by truly having an experience with the Word. Not only know it, but apply it. It's time to truly purge!

Pearls of Wisdom

- The notion of jumping into something new to get over something is a TRAP and unhealthy mechanism to truly deal with yourself, your past, your healing journey. Please don't fall for this trap! Take the time to be introspective, heal, and identify your patterns in relationships.
- Please please please I beg of you, give yourself time to heal! Evaluate the failed relationship, learn the lesson, change the patterns, change where you need to change, and do not rush into something else.
- Do not always blame others for the failed relationship but take an honest look at you, how you contribute, and what you can change. Now you are not doing this to make excuses for the other party or to go back to the failed relationship but to learn and see how you can do things differently! Again, let me remind you, abuse is NEVER your fault.
- Forgive yourself for the decisions you made, the fact you hurt other people, for wasting time and life, and for going back instead of moving forward! Extend to yourself compassion and thank the person you were to become the person you are emerging to be. This is a process—be gentle with yourself. "There is therefore now no condemnation to them which are in Christ Jesus, who walk not after the flesh, but after the Spirit (Romans 8:1 KJV).

Notes

_____

_____

_____

_____

_____

_____

Prayer

Father God,

I come to you to ask for forgiveness! Help me to forgive others and forgive myself. Sometimes this can be easier said than done. I need to release myself from my past, my mistakes, my wrong decisions, my failed relationships! I am not a failure, I'm not bad, I'm not my past, and I'm not the same version of me! Please heal those broken and failed places within me. Please remind me of my self worth and esteem. Please break every soul tie, every chain, close every hole, and every entryway the enemy will try to use to take me back.

Help me, Father, to remember YOU brought me OUT and set me FREE, and who the SON set free, is FREE INDEED! Holy Spirit, please restore me! Help me to set up healthy boundaries! Help me to recognize the patterns and deal with them. Help me to be proactive in my walk by not being drawn away by my own lust and desire. Help me to know your will for my life and help me intentionally and purposefully choose that! Thank you, God, for being a God of another chance and a new chance! I love you so much, and I'm grateful for you!

In Jesus Name,

Amen!

5. THE PURGE

How do you move on from 10 years of unsuccessful and failed relationships? Where do you start? Can this truly be a moment of time in the past?? Is there more?? These are all the questions I pondered. After years of heartbreak after heartbreak, I needed some true purging, cleansing, and healing. In this chapter I will focus on the purging and cleansing, and in the one to follow, I will discuss the process of healing.

The Merriam-Webster dictionary defines purging as "to rid something of whatever is impure or undesirable; cleanse; purify." The same dictionary defines cleansing specifically as "to rid something of impurities by or as if by washing clean the wound." Merriam Webster says clean and cleanse both mean "to free something of dirt or impurities." However, clean is used more generally to address everything from washing to tidying up. Cleanse is used more specifically to address removing dirt or germs, especially via washing, and is also used figuratively as seen in "cleanse the body/mind."(https://www.merriam-webster.com/words-at-play/clean-vs-cleanse-difference-usage)

When you have encountered years of toxic, unhealthy, unfaithful, or broken relationship, it is imperative and important you go through a cleansing and purging process. The process will help you get back on track. 2 Corinthians 7:1 (NLT)states "Because we have these promises, dear friends, let us cleanse ourselves from everything that can defile our body or spirit. And let us work toward complete holiness because we fear God."

The first step of my purging was receiving the revelation that this time I needed to truly work on me. I knew I didn't need to be in any other relationship until I purged from all the previous ones. I needed God to put it all back together again. In this phase of my life, I knew I needed God more than anything.

I have to say this, I knew God before and even when I was in the previous relationships. However, the reality is, I struggled. I struggled with choosing His will over my will. I struggled with choosing my desires over His desire. I allowed my struggles and the lust of my own flesh to rule my life. I knew God, but I did not allow Him to be in the driver's seat of my life. I thought I had a relationship with Him, but I still wanted to be in control. I was still conformed to the image of this world and needed a complete mind renewal. If I'm honest, even today I have to capture every thought that doesn't line up with God and surrender myself and my mind to Him daily!!

I knew the purging had to look different than what I did in the past. I needed accountability.

I moved to a new location, and I was living my dream of practicing law. Another real moment, I was successful in college, successful in law school, passed the bar. I was doing it BIG in other areas of my life but failing in the relationship department. While I was in this new area, I joined a local church. The teaching was rich, biblical, and pushed me to study God's word more.

While attending for a while, God reconnected me with a woman, Ms. JT, who became my accountability partner, intercessor, and midwife. Now, Ms. JT can be compared to one of those old mothers who sees beyond your smile and into your soul. God truly spoke through and used her to take me through this purging journey. She called out the brokenness in me and the wrong ways I tried to fix it. She was the first person who told me I needed to purge and cleanse myself. She not only told me, but she shared with me how and what that looked like.

She told to me cut off any contacts with the opposite sex. This was huge because even though I was not in a relationship, I still had old contacts that, if I wanted, I could hit up. I still had access to people who, if I felt like I needed conversation or even to go on a date, I could.

When she told me to separate, I initially thought it didn't take all of that. I could keep a few numbers just in case. But let me tell you, it was like God gave her access to my phone and messages. She would know if I had entertained a phone conversation or went on a date. I grew tired of the rebukes and her calling me out. So I listened, and I went on this journey where God started to truly deal with me, the real me.

God used this lady to help me deal with my parents' divorce, my relationship baggage, my insecurities, rejection, and abandonment issues. She would call me at 5 a.m. to cover me in prayer. She stayed praying for me, loving me, and holding me accountable. She also was preparing me for what God had planned for me.

In this phase of my life, God was my everything, and He was enough. I stayed in my word. I read countless books on praying, intercession, relationship with God, and healing. I was asked to join the prayer team at church and a prayer ministry that my spiritual mentor, Robbie, started. God was purging me, freeing me, loving me. God was showing me who I was in Him. He surrounded me with women who loved him, too, and were sold out to Him. Then he started healing me.

The purging is a crucial part of your healing process. I want to stress a few key points that helped me and can assist you on your purging journey. During your purge, it is imperative to have seasoned mentors who are mature in their lives and can help assist you in your journey. This person (or these people) needs to be connected to God and have a strong relationship with Him. They should be trustworthy, wise, graceful, loving, and able to truly push you through your season. Vet this person before you choose them.

The next step is separating yourself from soul ties. In Chapter 1, I spoke about how I not only had to separate myself from the person, but I had to burn everything that would remind me of him. I also had to purge myself from all sexual connections to him. It is imperative to truly sever the ties and block the connection. You cannot stop there! It is important to have a safe space where you can share and be transparent about your struggles, your testimony, your journey, and even your desire for different. This safe haven is where you can be open and honest about your experience.

Finally, but not least, find yourself a bible-based church, get involved by serving a need, and surround yourself with other believers and like-minded friends who are committed to pleasing and serving God.

All of these things are important because when temptation comes, and the enemy comes, which we know he will because he stays on the prowl to steal, kill, and destroy, you can be ready! Not only that, you have surrounded yourself with a spiritual army that can help you. "Two are better than one, because they have a good return for their labor: If either of them falls down, one can help the other up. But pity anyone who falls and has no one to help them up." (NIV, Eccles 4:9-10)

Pearls of Wisdom

- Godly Accountability is much needed! Regardless of how society or people will entertain this notion of being solo, that is a lie and device of the enemy. You need people, you need accountability, and you need sound, wise counsel!
- Purging and cleansing from the past, regardless of your story, is necessary for your future! This process looks different for everyone.
- The WORD of God still works! You will find strength in the word, Peace in the word, Healing in the word, Comfort in the Word! Everything you need in every phase you are in life can be found in the word of God, his holy book, the Bible!

Notes

_____

_____

_____

_____

_____

_____

_____

_____

_____

_____

_____

_____

_____

_____

Prayer

God,

Thank you so much for the PURGE! Purge us, dear Lord, to make us new and more like you! Thank you so much for godly connections! Thank you so much for giving me spiritual mentors such as Mrs. Cade-Furdge and Ms. JT, who have walked this life and are still walking this life out with me. You have given me women who pick me up in the spirit, uplift me, and intercede on my behalf. I pray a special blessing over them for this!

God, I pray that you reveal the right accountability for all of your children. And remind them the importance of connection, accountability and how sound, wise counsel can help us, protect us, and catapult us. Also, give us ears and a heart to listen and take heed to wise counsel even when it's hard and we do not want to do it!

God, give us a hunger and a thirst for you and your word! Help us to understand the power that is in it and how it is living and True! Help us to not be only hearers but doers of your word(James 1:22-25)! Thank you, God!

In Christ's Mighty name,

Amen!

6. The Wait

Now I know some of you may be wondering, *What's the difference between purging and healing?*

Healing is defined by the Oxford English dictionary as "the process of making or becoming sound or healthy again."

Purging was the first step of my healing process. I had to rid myself of all the negativity rid myself of the things that had to stop, rid myself of the brokenness.

When I think about purging, I think about getting rid of all the toxins in the body before you can start healing, like a detox cleanse. That's exactly what was going on. God was cleansing me of all the toxins, all the unproductive ways, all the places I wasn't growing-pruning, and all the bad thinking and negative perspectives in order to work in me.

Healing takes things a step further and a level deeper.

The illustration I think of when it comes to the healing process came straight from my husband. He told me, "Different wounds require different kinds of healing." When you have to be healed from a scratch or a scab, you are likely to put some ointment on it, a bandage, and the healing will occur soon thereafter.

But the healing process from a tear or break takes a lot longer and more attention. With a tear or a break, you have to give yourself the necessary time and space to heal. The process can be anywhere from six weeks to months. There are other organs that are working together to get the muscles to heal or the bones to heal. But you have to take it a step further, and you have to see a doctor. After seeing a doctor, you most likely have to see a physical therapist to help you strengthen that muscle or bone to get it back into working condition.

I wasn't just getting healed from a scratch or scab, but I had some tears and brokenness. I needed the great Doctor, my God. I also needed some therapy from a counselor to help me navigate.

The first step of my healing was forgiveness. I could not truly heal until I forgave. One night while in prayer, I asked God who I needed to forgive. I wrote out a list of people who have hurt me, betrayed me, and broken me. Even though I was in my twenties, God took me back to my childhood to deal with past hurt. I had to forgive the man who took one of the most precious things away from me without my consent, I had to forgive my first boyfriend for breaking my heart when I gave him the very thing that I thought would not be taken for granted, I had to forgive childhood friends who were not really friends, forgive the guy I decided to take another chance with love, and he hurt me, and finally I had to forgive myself.

With some of these people, God had me actually making contact to let them know they hurt me and I forgave them. God also dealt with others, and they came to me to ask for forgiveness.

I think the hardest part was forgiving myself. I've made so many mistakes, so many bad choices, and even hurt others because I was hurt. Hurting others while being hurt is inevitable. I've heard people say we are hardest on ourselves, and this is true.

A part of me felt like I didn't deserve to be forgiven. That's when God dealt with my heart. It felt like he performed heart surgery on me, taking out the cold, hardened heart, and giving me a new one. He forgave me and cast my sins and wrongdoing in a sea of forgetfulness. If the King of Kings, my creator, could forgive me, then why couldn't I forgive myself? It was vital for me to forgive me. It was freeing and liberating to forgive me. No longer bound by my past, but free because the Son Jesus made me free.

I've always been a person who loves to smile, even when I was at the worst moments in my life, but this time I could truly smile and it was REAL—it was my true expression.

After forgiving others and myself, God had me in a place where I was able to be transparent with others and confess the things I've been through and done. I was being healed even further by my testimony and sharing my testimony.

The next step in healing is believing you are healed and walking in it. When the enemy, the negative thoughts and the negative talk, comes, you have to stand firm on your faith and believe you are healed.

I have to say this now—things will come up and may trigger you. When you experience those triggers, it just means you have to deal with another layer of the hurt, but it doesn't mean you are not healed. Ask God to help and strengthen you during the trigger. Also, when things come up in your mind and heart, take captive of every thought and make it come under subjection to what God has already said about you and done for you.

Walk in your healing, even when it is hard. Walk in your healing, even when you feel defeated. Walk in your healing and forgiveness, even when similar situations rear their ugly heads. Walk in your healing knowing whom the son sets free is free indeed.

The last step of healing is getting people around you to cover you in prayer and who can speak truth to you in love.

The healing process is more manageable when you have people in your corner. This is not the time to shun those people but to depend on them.

One thing about our society that I hate to see, is that the fact that people tend to shun therapy and counseling. Counseling is and continues to be a really good resource. IT IS OKAY that we see a therapist. It should not be looked at as a stigma but as a beneficial resource. Therapy, pre- and post-marital counseling, and confiding in spiritual leaders have helped me beyond words. I honestly felt a load come off when I had my therapy sessions. I went into therapy for one thing, and by the end of it, I had shared my whole life story and left feeling so light!

- Healing, true Healing is so vital to your well being. In order to truly be your WHOLE self, you have to heal!
- Healing process start with Forgiveness. Forgiving others who hurt, betrayed, mistreated, and misused you. Also, Forgive Yourself!
- It's okay to have Jesus, Holy Spirit, and a Therapist! There are things we can get through in life by prayer and supplication but there are things and times we need to really seek out counseling and a therapist to help get through our traumas.

Notes

_____

_____

_____

_____

_____

_____

_____

_____

_____

_____

_____

_____

_____

_____

Prayer

Jehovah Rophe, the one who heals!

We come to you our ultimate healer! First, asking for forgiveness for our sins, our wrongdoing, and how we have hurt others. Help us to forgive ourselves; also forgive those who have hurt us. We understand forgiveness is the first step for our healing journey. We ask for healing also, Father!

Your son was wounded for our transgressions, he was bruised for our iniquities: **the chastisement of our peace was upon him; and with his stripes we are healed** (Isa53:5 KJV). Thank you, Jesus, for all you've done for us and that we can receive healing because of you!

God, I pray for all of those who are reading and will read this book. I pray for healing from hurt, brokenness, wounds, trauma, insecurities, rejection, people, words, and anything and everything that has caused us pain and hurt. God, I cover physical illness and sickness that has been caused over the years due to trauma, unhealedness, bitterness, resentment, failures, stress, overwhelmedness, and life! God, I pray that you go beyond the layers, triggers, and surface to heal us.

God, please help us discern and know when we need to seek out counseling and a therapist. Help us not to be ashamed but reveal the benefits to us.

God, help us to be surrounded by the right people who will push us towards healing and not those who remind us of our defeat.

God, we submit our healing process to you and give you full reign. Thank you, God, that we are healed and Whole people!

In Jesus Mighty and Holy Name,

Amen!

7. The Turnaround

Have you ever attended an intense workout class or even a boot camp? The class is so intense, you are exhausted. You feel good because you completed the work, but it definitely took a toll. I remember when I was training with a trainer. It was boot camp twice or even three times a week. Every time I would leave that class, I felt like I was going to vomit. I would sit in my car after that class and just breathe.

If you have experienced that, the feeling is similar to my purging, cleansing, and healing process. It was intenseeeeeeee! I mean, I felt like I put in major work, and I was exhausted. But I felt good and like it was necessary!

After this intense phase of my life, where I felt like God had lined up everything, He started dealing with the relationship part of my life. As I said, I was crushing every other area, but the relationship area needed work.

I believe one of the reasons that this part failed is because I didn't have a solid relationship with Christ first. I didn't allow Him to help me wholeheartedly in this area. I first had to shift the purpose! It wasn't about a man, but it was about the God man, my Father, Jesus Christ! He wanted all of me first and forever. I got it wrong because I was giving him pieces of me instead of all of me. Not only did He want me giving Him all of me, but I also should have been asking Him for his wisdom and guidance concerning every area including relationships. As a single woman, I needed to make sure before I got into anything serious that my relationship with God was serious, first, and solid! As a single believer my first important purpose is to be a vessel for Him in this earth. I needed to be about my Father's business. Whatever pleased Him should please me and be first in my life. When I got to that point, God started preparing my heart for marriage.

This chapter is not at all about marriage, but it's about God's new beginning for me in every area. Growing up, I had seen a lot of failed marriages, so it was something I didn't think I wanted. But God changed my heart and perspective! Their story was not my story, and I couldn't take their story on! I remember the day that God gave me a glimpse of his promises for me.

One evening, I was heading to this conference, and I was listening to my spiritual mentor, Robbie, teaching a sermon about the three Ps... Being connected to the right purpose, place, and position. At the end of the message, she challenged the listeners to seek God and ask him the three Ps concerning our lives. So I turned off everything in my car as I was driving. I asked God to reveal me the three Ps for my life! I sought Him and got still before Him. After praying, all I kept hearing Him say was "Detroit" and the number 320. I didn't know what any of that meant, but I knew He would reveal it to me soon.

Weeks later, I was at a women's retreat and a minister told me my husband was not in Monroe, which was where I lived at the time, but he was miles away in Detroit. I'm thinking, "Do I know anyone from Detroit?" Even with this word, I continue to do what I was doing—seeking God, pursuing Him, and grinding in my career. During this time, I was still on a spiritual journey where I was not dating anyone, I was not entertaining anyone, and I was celibate.

I finally was in a place where I felt like I was right where I was supposed to be in life. I felt like God had healed me, and He was teaching me how to live a whole life and a life to please Him. I knew I was healed because everything I once depended on had been stripped away and I totally relied on God! I knew I was healed because my heart no longer felt numb, but it desired to love and I felt like I had the capacity to love! I knew I was healed because I'd done the work to heal so now I was just walking into that healing. The healing journey was a freeing one! I no longer felt bound by my past or mistakes but I released it!

While being in this place for almost a year, something amazing happened. My friend/mentor Robbie had made a connection. She introduced me to one of her good guy friends. Guess where he was located???? In Detroit, Michigan. So, after the introduction, we became friends. We started conversing on Facebook messenger, and then we exchanged numbers after he told me he was intrigued by me and wanted to see where things could go. I helped him start his company, we did devotions together, and we truly helped each other to become deeper in Christ.

We both had been in a long-term relationship in the past that did not work. So even though he pursued me, he soon thereafter friendzoned me. I discovered one of the main reasons was because he was not 100 percent sure if he was ready to be in a relationship. So we stayed in the friend zone for a while.

After developing a deep friendship for seven months, we decided to start dating. While we were dating, he started to build a house in Virginia, his home state, where the last three digits of his zip code were 320—and that was the number God had given me almost a year before while I was listening to that 3 P Message.

We did not date long, maybe 9 months before he proposed. Then we were married about 10 months after that. Things truly moved because we both were confident that this was a God thing! I have so much I want to share concerning our journey, but I will stop here. We will share our love story in a book we are working on together and some tips we have learned over the course of our marriage.

After you have had a glimpse of a solid, good relationship and a genuine good guy, you recognize what's good for you and what's not. You notice you don't have to settle instead— or cast your pearls before SWINE, or give your time and energy to unhealthy, unfruitful relationships. You find you're confident in waiting on God.

There are great guys out there so there's no need to settle, even when it feels like there's a slim chance of meeting one. God can and will prepare a husband just for you especially when it is HIS Will.

Beware of the red flags, don't spend years in a toxic, unhealthy situation, and when you see those patterns, don't settle for potential or think you can change a person. Also, if you are reading this right now, and in this moment, you recognize you are in a toxic situation or see the unhealthy pattern, it's not too late to change and make a shift.

If you are desiring to be healed and whole, I encourage you to lay all of you, your hurt, brokenness, pain, anger, disappointment, and everything, at our Father's feet and allow Him to do a work within you! Make a conscious decision to choose healing and walk in it. Remember nothing is too hard for God! Keep trusting Him for your turnaround and your new beginning.

- God can change the trajectory of your entire life and different areas of your life! Nothing is too hard or impossible with God!
- Healing is available to all of us. He healed me and so many, so He can heal you!
- It can be easy to lose focus or focus on the wrong thing, but as long as you have breath in your body, God can shift your focus and can align your focus with His focus.

Notes

_____

_____

_____

_____

_____

_____

_____

_____

_____

_____

_____

_____

_____

Prayers

Thank you, Father!

Thank you for being a God who loves and cares for every area of our life. Thank you that nothing is Impossible with you! You can make All things possible. God, help us to recognize that you have all power in your hand, and you can change things on our behalf.

Thank you, God, for ordained messages that change us, and thanks for pastors, leaders, and ministers who equip and help us. God, before we choose to have a relationship with anyone, help us to have a solid relationship with you. Help us to first give our lives our gifts and talents, our all to you. Help us to daily fulfill the purposes you have called us to.

God, thank you for changing my perspectives on marriage and relationships and giving me Hope!

God, thank you for my husband and our marriage. I cover marriages this day. That couples will be reminded to cover one another in prayer and keep you as a viable chord in their marriage. God, show and remind couples that marriage is a reflection of what Jesus has done for us. You take two imperfect people, join them in a covenant to show the WORLD a perfect love, the love that You have for it. Marriage becomes an example of your love to a sinful world. You take the husband as a typology of Christ to show the characteristic of Christ. What was Christ's purpose? He died for a sinful world to save us from death and eternal hell. The man (husband) has to be willing to love his wife like Christ love the church to the point that he is willing to die. The bride represents the church. The woman (bride) is supposed to honor, revere, respect, and submit to her OWN husband. By doing so, she exemplifies love. In essence, marriage is an opportunity for two people to join together solely for the purpose to glorify You. Also, it's a symbol of your glory and your love.

You put together imperfect people through a Holy Union to carry out a specific purpose. Help us to carry out the purpose you desire for our marriage and for your glory. Help us to please you with our marriage. Help us to put away our own selfish desire to please you.

We love you and Amen.

8. Conclusion

I want to end this book saying, sometimes people look at you now and don't know the backstory. I truly hope that this book helps you and provides you with some tips that will shift your paradigm. Also, I've encountered my share of ups and downs, but through it all, God has helped, healed, and kept me. He placed a burden on my heart to share my story to help others to be free, healed, and whole. As scripture says in Revelation, we are healed by the blood of the Lamb and the word of our testimony! I am a pretty private person, especially if you do not know me, but I want to truly be a vessel. I want to share my journey and keys, and if it helps one person, my job is close to being done.

With that being said, I know we all have had our share of good, bad, or ugly. I know our testimonies can have some similar elements but I want to encourage you. Choose to be victorious and Healed! Don't live in the victim mindset. The mindset that says *because of these bad things that happened to me, I am only that or the result of it*. Because if you choose that story, you will walk in that story forever! But once you choose the opposite, *it happened to me, I'm not that or a victim. God has healed me and I can walk in that freedom*— there's strength, healing, and liberty there!

I do not want you to take anything from this book as an excuse or a crutch, but as a journey that had some ups, downs, and bumps. But it did not end there! God used all of those things to make, mold, and shape me into who I am today.

What I have learned is that God was with me even when I left him or thought the opposite.

Do not look down on your journey or even your present situation BUT CHOOSE different, CHOOSE his PERFECT WILL for your life and not just settled for the potential of GOOD!

One of the major keys I want you to get from this book is to choose healing and forgiveness. We all have experienced different kinds of trauma, whether from childhood, teen years, or adulthood but we cannot allow ourselves to live and die in that trauma. We have to choose healing, wholeness, and freedom. The first step is choosing, and after that is putting some steps in place to walk in it and live in it. Those steps depend on you, but I have given you some major keys in this book to assist you on your journey. Also, please know I am here. I am not a professional counselor or therapist but I can tell you my testimony and share more of my victories to help you! Please reach out, and especially if I can provide you with some resources to help you get out of a stagnated or toxic situation.

Final Prayer

My God, My Father, My Healer, and Deliver!!

Thank you so much for everything you are and have been to me. God, I want to cover all the readers! Some readers will be coming out, going through, or even in the midst of different situations, and I pray that you meet them right where they are. Remind them who you created them to be before they entered into the womb.

God, help them to heal, be free, be delivered, and live the life you have for them. Help them to not choose toxic, unhealthy relationships, regardless if they are romantic or friendships!

God, order their steps so that they will not settle for things that are not in YOUR WILL for them. God, please help them to TRUST IN YOU with all their Hearts, Minds, and Strength and Acknowledge YOU in all their ways! God, please do not leave nor forsake any of them. Remind them of their value, their victory through you, their worth, and Your love! Help them not to get stuck.

God, I pray that every word that has been written is protected and accomplishes what you will have it do. You already know who would read this book and what they need from it—minister, dear Lord, like only you can!

I thank you in advance for what you are doing and about to do! I appreciate you and love you!

In Jesus name,

Amen

About the Author

LaKeisha Carey is originally from Bernice, Louisiana and raised by her father Victor Gray in the beautiful community of Bernice, Louisiana. God implanted in Keisha the aspiration of becoming a lawyer when she was in sixth grade.

She graduated Bernice High School in 2004 as Valedictorian. Then she went to college at Northwestern State University (NSU) on scholarship and majored in Pre-Law/Criminal Justice. She graduated from (NSU) as Magna Cumme Laude. Also, she graduated from Southern University Law Center Fall 2011 in the top 5 percent of her graduating class. From 2011-2014, she was a practicing attorney representing children.

During that time, she became a new children's book author; the book is titled *"Cankeyo" You Can Keep Your Dreams Alive!*

She married the love of her life, Don J Carey III on June 28, 2014 in New Orleans, Louisiana.

They started their own nonprofit called the Don Carey REECH (Reaching, Educating, and Empowering Children) Foundation and Lakeisha became the Executive Director of the Don Carey REECH Foundation in 2017.

The Don Carey REECH Foundation believes that providing students the opportunity of academic achievement and exposure to diverse arenas, they can ultimately be inspired to reach their maximum potential and become significant contributors to society. Specifically, in the areas of literacy, STEM, physical wellbeing, health, social and moral responsibility along with vocational and collegiate preparation. Check out the website at www.reechfoundation.org.

Lakeisha and Don have three beautiful children, two sons, Victor and Asher, and one daughter, Amelia.

Lakeisha is the founder and owner of Carey Consultant Firm where she helps individual actualize their dreams by building their businesses and/or nonprofits. Also, at her firm, she handles Wills and Estate, Workers Compensation, and General Practice areas.